The Secret House of Papa Mouse

Please visit our web site at: www.garethstevens.com
For a free color catalog describing Gareth Stevens Publishing's
list of high-quality books and multimedia programs, call
1-800-542-2595 (USA) or 1-800-387-3178 (Canada).
Gareth Stevens Publishing's fax: (414) 332-3567.

Library of Congress Cataloging-in-Publication Data

Landa, Norbert.
    [Bei Maus Zu Haus, English]
    The secret house of Papa Mouse / by Norbert Landa; illustrations by Hanne Türk.
        p. cm.
    Summary: Tucked away in the attic of an apartment building, each room of the
    Mouse family's house is furnished with familiar household objects that have been taken
    from the people who live below.
    ISBN 0-8368-4106-9 (lib. bdg.)
    [1. Mice—Fiction. 2. Dwellings—Fiction.] I. Türk, Hanne, ill. II. Title.
    PZ7.L23165Se   2004
    [E]—dc22   2004045323

This North American edition first published in 2005 by
Gareth Stevens Publishing
A World Almanac Education Group Company
330 West Olive Street, Suite 100
Milwaukee, Wisconsin 53212 USA

Original text copyright © 2001 Norbert Landa.
Original illustrations copyright © 2001 Hanne Türk.
Original German edition published by Fleurus Verlag.
German text: Norbert Landa
Illustrations: Hanne Türk
Photos: Fotografikdesign Weber & Göröcs
Book design: Yulia Vershinskaya
World rights reserved

This U.S. edition copyright © 2005 by Gareth Stevens, Inc.
English translation: Monica Rausch
English text: Dorothy L. Gibbs
Gareth Stevens art direction: Tammy West

Printed in the United States of America

1 2 3 4 5 6 7 8 9 08 07 06 05 04

The Secret House of Papa Mouse

Norbert Landa

Hanne Türk

GARETH**STEVENS**

GS

PUBLISHING

A World Almanac Education Group Company

The apartments lining Pleasant Street are homes to many families, but folks who live in one of them are puzzled by these mysteries:

"Where's my comb?" asks Mrs. Quinn.
"An eggcup's missing, too!"

"And I can't find," her husband sighed, "the brush to shine my shoe."

The lady in apartment six was missing quite a bit: thimbles, thread, a metal box — her favorite oven mitt.

Some marbles from Bob's bag are gone! Could they have rolled away? A puzzle's missing pieces now. Peg saw them yesterday.

Ben searches for his ballpoint pen to write a book report. A brand new deck of playing cards has turned up four cards short.

From family to family, the little girls and boys claimed dominoes and shuttlecocks were missing from their toys.

Everyone was unaware that, with them in the house, lived another family — a family named "Mouse."

High beneath the attic roof, the mice had eight small rooms, a terrace, and a workshop they kept clean with little brooms.

Their furniture was made from things, all taken late at night, when Papa Mouse went prowling, snatching everything in sight.

Bottle caps and buttons, paper clips and postage stamps made dandy household items, from beds to hanging lamps.

The oven mitt from number six is now a comfy chair. The eggcup's now a planter, and some parsley's growing there.

Only Papa Mouse and Papa's little family know about their secret house — but you can come and see!

As you visit Papa's rooms
(all pictured in this book),
try to find the missing things.

Come in and take a look . . .

Good morning!

It's morning at the house of "Mouse," and Papa's on his way to eat.
Do you recognize the rug that's stretched out underneath his feet?

shampoo bottle cap	postage stamps	hair comb	pencil sharpener	paper umbrellas
screw	string	makeup brush	ribbon	pearls
bottle cap	powder brush	paper candy cup	cream container	hairpin
tea light tins	coin purse	plastic screw anchor	hair clips	colored pencil

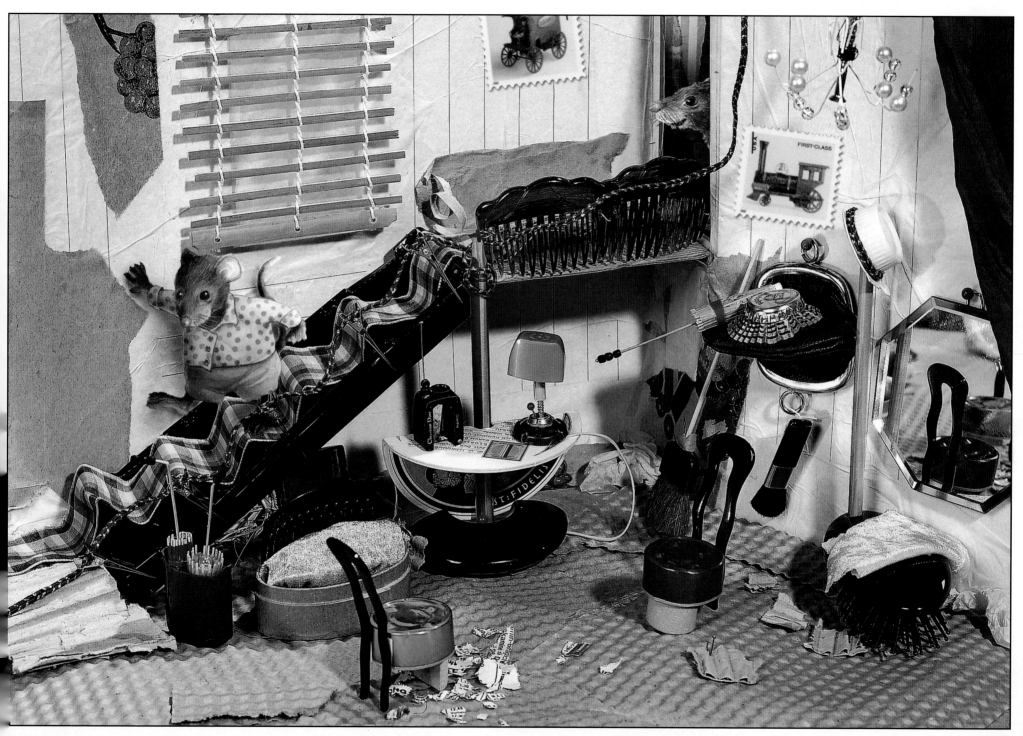

In the kitchen

After breakfast, Papa cleans. When mice eat, they make quite a mess. Look!
There's the missing shoe-shine brush. What else was missing? Can you guess?

 walnut shells	 safety pin	 toothbrush head	 staples	buttons
 chopsticks	 funnel	 tea light tin	tea tin	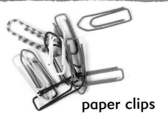 paper clips
 porcelain baking dish	puzzle pieces	 place mat	thimble	 paper candy cup
 shoe brushes	 pump dispenser bottle top	 metal jar lid	 plastic bottle caps	metal canister

In the office

Papa's in his office now. He is a working mouse, you see.
As you search for missing things, be sure you do it quietly.

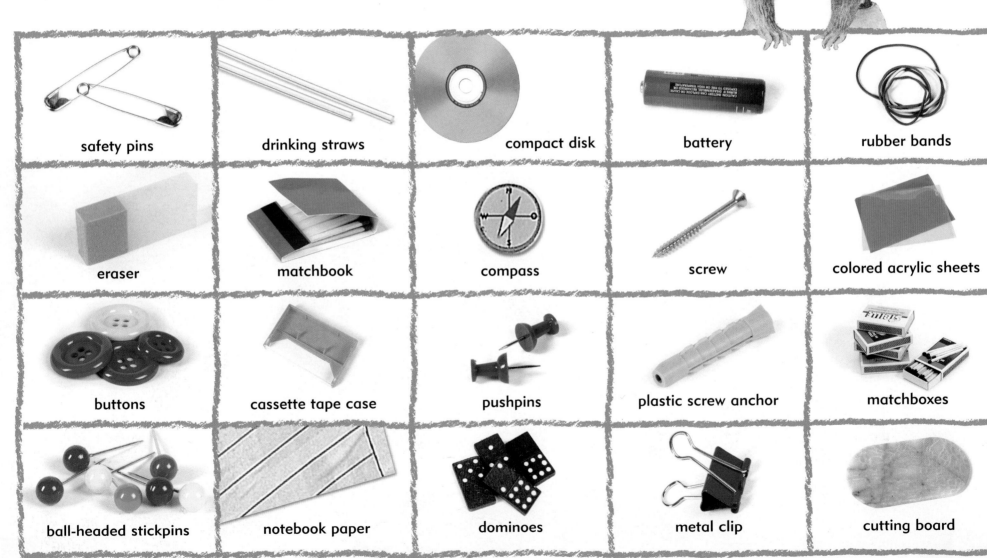

safety pins	drinking straws	compact disk	battery	rubber bands
eraser	matchbook	compass	screw	colored acrylic sheets
buttons	cassette tape case	pushpins	plastic screw anchor	matchboxes
ball-headed stickpins	notebook paper	dominoes	metal clip	cutting board

In the children's room

While Papa works, his children play. The little mice have toys galore!
Do you see the dominoes? Are those Bob's marbles on the floor?

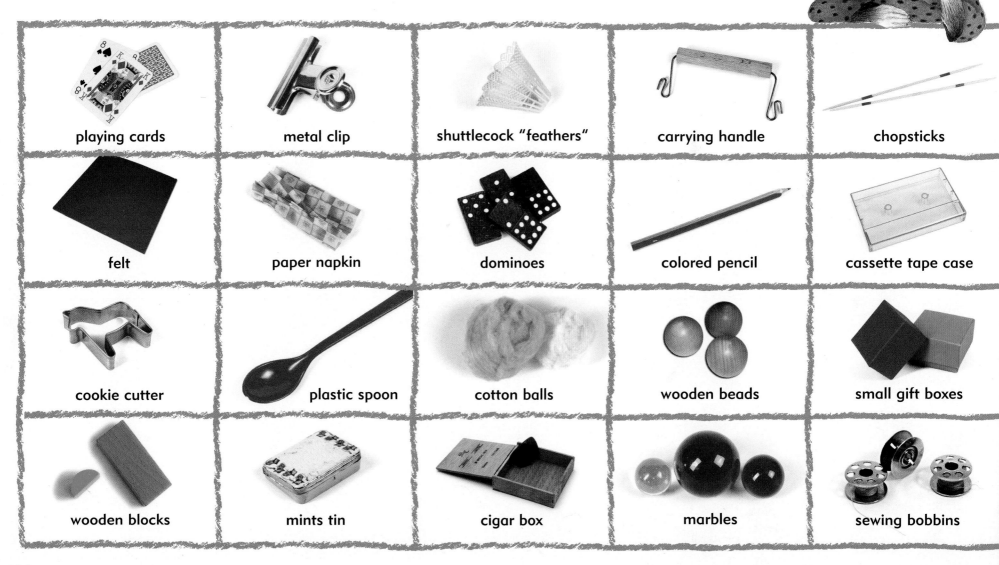

playing cards	metal clip	shuttlecock "feathers"	carrying handle	chopsticks
felt	paper napkin	dominoes	colored pencil	cassette tape case
cookie cutter	plastic spoon	cotton balls	wooden beads	small gift boxes
wooden blocks	mints tin	cigar box	marbles	sewing bobbins

In the living room

Papa's going to read the news and watch a mouse show on TV.
In his cozy living room, which missing objects do you see?

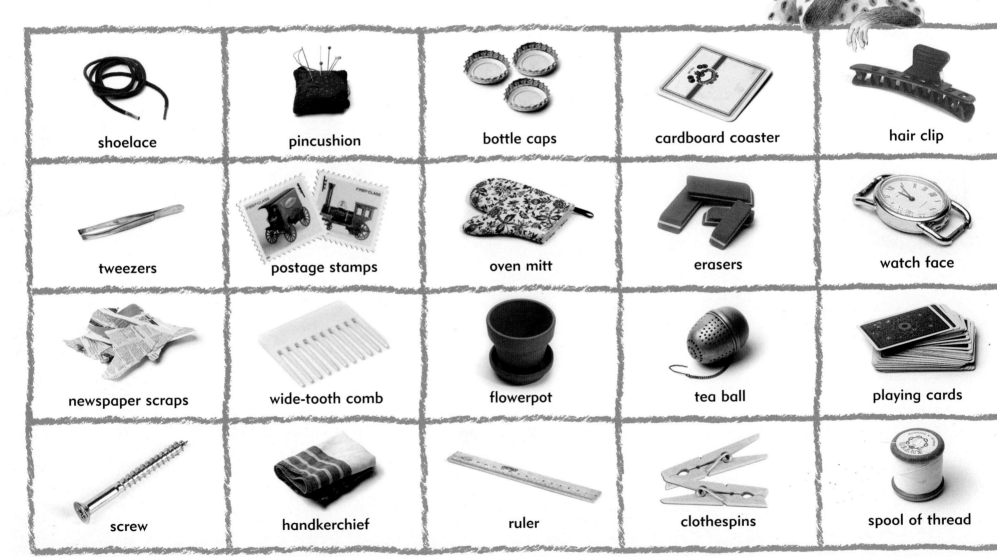

shoelace	pincushion	bottle caps	cardboard coaster	hair clip
tweezers	postage stamps	oven mitt	erasers	watch face
newspaper scraps	wide-tooth comb	flowerpot	tea ball	playing cards
screw	handkerchief	ruler	clothespins	spool of thread

In the fitness room

Even mice, although they're small, work out so they don't get too fat.
They pedal on a "button" bike — do sit-ups on a "flat sponge" mat.

 plastic bottle caps	 buttons	pencil sharpener	 cotton swabs	 elastic hair bands
hair clips	 chopsticks	empty cellophane tape roll	 sponge	 pencil case
 dominoes	 mesh tea strainer	 staples	 cassette tape case	 wrench
 matchboxes	 tea bag	 flat sponge	 spring from a ballpoint pen	wire top from a champagne bottle

On the terrace

To get fresh air, the mice go to their little terrace on the roof
that Papa made with many things from the apartments — here is proof!

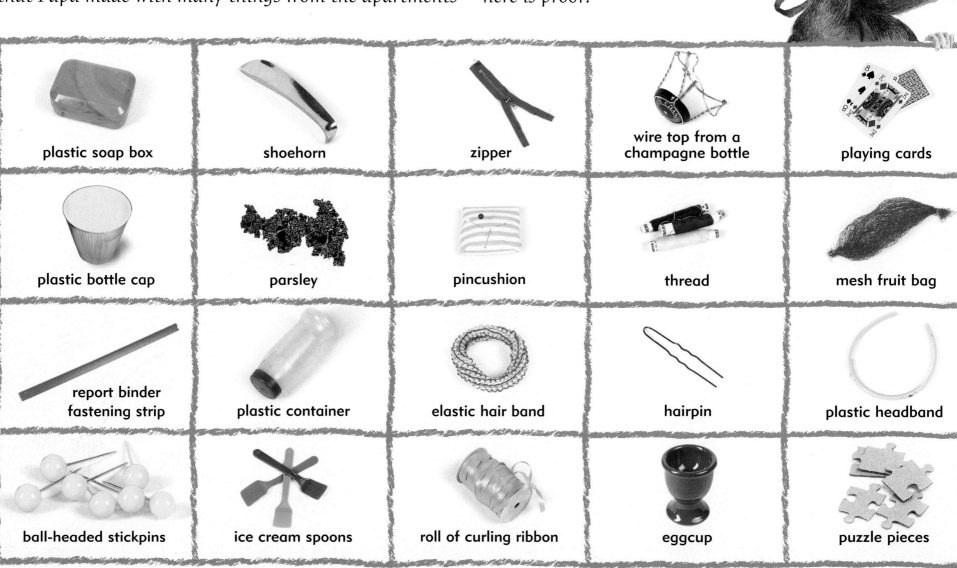

plastic soap box	shoehorn	zipper	wire top from a champagne bottle	playing cards
plastic bottle cap	parsley	pincushion	thread	mesh fruit bag
report binder fastening strip	plastic container	elastic hair band	hairpin	plastic headband
ball-headed stickpins	ice cream spoons	roll of curling ribbon	eggcup	puzzle pieces

In the workshop

Of all the rooms in Papa's house, his workshop is his pride and joy.
Do you see what Papa used to make his little mice a toy?

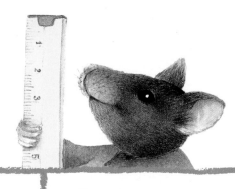

 rubber bands	 clothespins	 buttons	 sink stopper	 plastic screw anchor
 nail	pencil sharpener	 cookie cutter	 adhesive bandage	padlock
 matchbox	 film canister	 staples	 battery	 measuring spoon
 metal canister lid	 spring from a ballpoint pen	sewing bobbin	 thread	safety pin

In the bathroom

Mouse fur can get dirty whether mice are hard at work or play.
All the things you see below will help these mice wash dirt away.

drinking straws	butter dish	shuttlecock	soap dish	plastic freezer bag
paper clips	eggcup	sewing bobbin	hanging clip	spring from a ballpoint pen
hair roller	seashells	nail file	flat sponge	lid of a salt shaker
cream container	pocket mirror	toothpicks	bubble wrap	toothbrush head

In the bedroom

After baths, it's time for bed. Here's Papa's bedroom (to the right).
A mattress made of cotton balls keeps Mama comfortable all night.

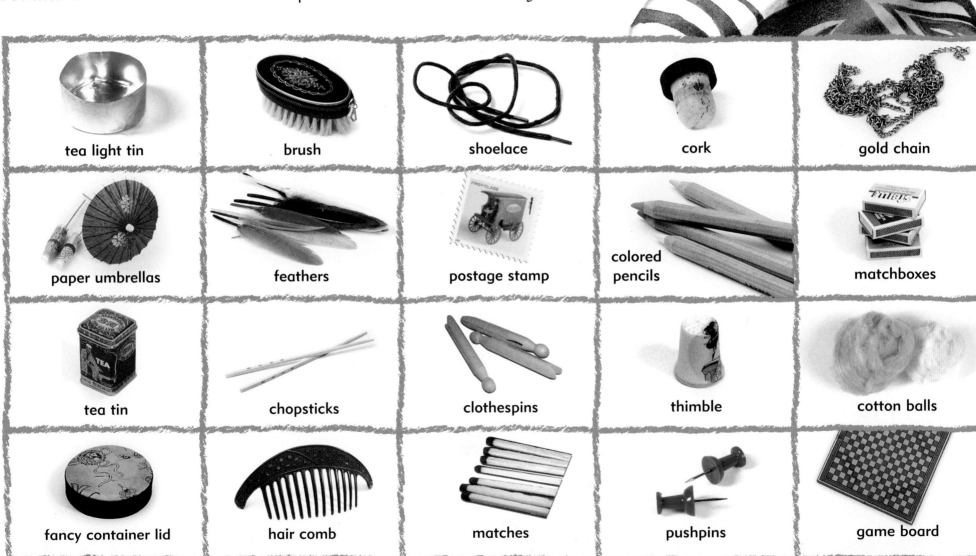

tea light tin	brush	shoelace	cork	gold chain
paper umbrellas	feathers	postage stamp	colored pencils	matchboxes
tea tin	chopsticks	clothespins	thimble	cotton balls
fancy container lid	hair comb	matches	pushpins	game board

Papa sleeps, but only till the middle of the night, when he makes his rounds again, with his bag and light. If you're awake, you'll see him tiptoe softly down each stair, then scamper through apartments while the folks sleep — unaware.

He'll pick up every little thing that he can use to make new furniture, accessories, or even chocolate cake!

Mama wakes to wish him luck, then, without a peep, Papa's gone a-prowling, and Mama's fast asleep. She's dreaming of the fine new things her husband, Papa Mouse, will bring back in the morning to their lovely secret house.

It's nighttime now on Pleasant Street,
but, as night turns to day, the folks will
wake and brush their teeth, and, soon,
you'll hear them say:

"What's happened to my rollers? How
will I curl my hair?"

"My thimble's gone! I've looked, but I
can't find it anywhere."

"Who used up all the bandages? I've
cut my fingertip."

"I finished my report for school but
need a paper clip!"

And as the folks are scurrying around and
getting dressed, Papa Mouse is settling into
bed. He needs a rest!

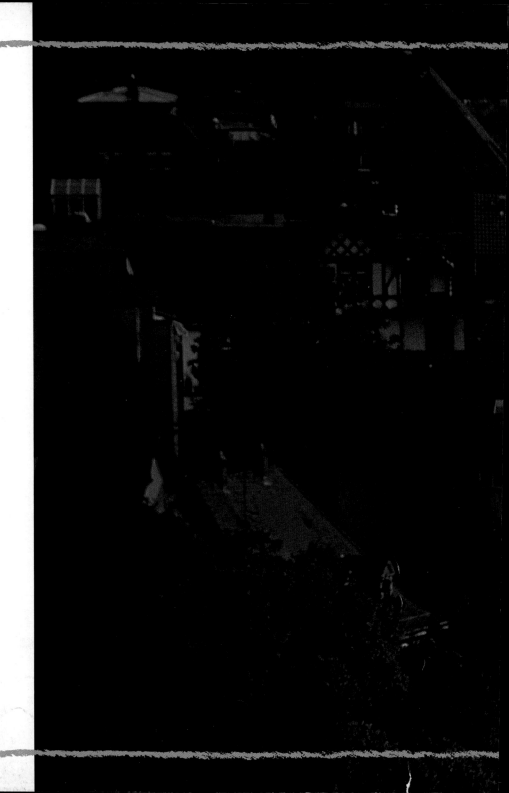